Contents

Any words appearing in the text in bold, **like this**,
are explained in the Glossary.

What is a rat?

Most people think of rats as nasty wild animals that live in sewers and spread diseases. So do not be surprised if people ask you how you could possibly want to keep a rat as a pet!

But are pet rats really so horrible? The answer is, not a bit! Pet rats are not the same as wild rats that **scavenge**, or hunt for food, in rubbish tips or sewers. They have been **domesticated** for many years so they now make excellent and friendly pets.

Wild rats often live on rubbish tips. They survive by eating anything they can find.

4

Rats in history

Pet rats have a history that goes back hundreds of years. Grand ladies of fashion in the 1800s kept attractive coloured rats as pets. These were probably just unusually coloured wild rats caught by rat catchers. But people came to realize that rats could make affectionate, intelligent pets.

Famous rats

One of the most famous pet rats was a white rat called Sammy. Sammy belonged to Beatrix Potter, the author of the Peter Rabbit stories.

Many people think that rats are the best small pets for adults and children.

Need to know

- Wild rats are classed as **vermin**, or **pests**. It is **illegal** to keep vermin so you must not take rats from the wild.
- Domesticated rats should not be allowed to **breed** with wild rats or be released into the wild.
- Children are not allowed to buy pets themselves. In any case, you should always have an adult with you when you buy your pets.
- Most countries have laws protecting animals. It is your responsibility to make sure your rats are healthy and well cared for. Always take your pets to the vet if they are ill or have been injured.

Rat facts

Rats are **mammals**. This means they are **warm-blooded** creatures (they produce their own body heat) which give birth to their young and feed their babies with milk. They are members of the **rodent** family, which includes mice, rabbits, guinea pigs, hamsters and gerbils. In fact, quite a lot of small pets are rodents! All rodents have long teeth for gnawing. A rat's teeth grow throughout its life so rats need to gnaw to keep their teeth short. If their teeth grow too long, they can die of starvation because they cannot eat properly.

Rats are members of the rodent family. Like all rodents, they will gnaw on things to keep their teeth short.

Did you know?

- Rats live for around two to three years.
- Male rats are called **bucks**.
- Female rats are called **does**.
- Young rats are called **kittens** (and also, occasionally, 'pups').
- Male rats can weigh up to 600 grams.
- Female rats weigh between 200 and 300 grams.
- A rat's tail may be as long as its body.

Rat babies

Rats **mature**, or grow up, very quickly and can have babies of their own when they are only two or three months old. This is one reason why rats can be such **pests** in the wild. Rats have lots of babies in a **litter**. They can have several litters in a year, by which time the babies will have grown up enough to have babies of their own!

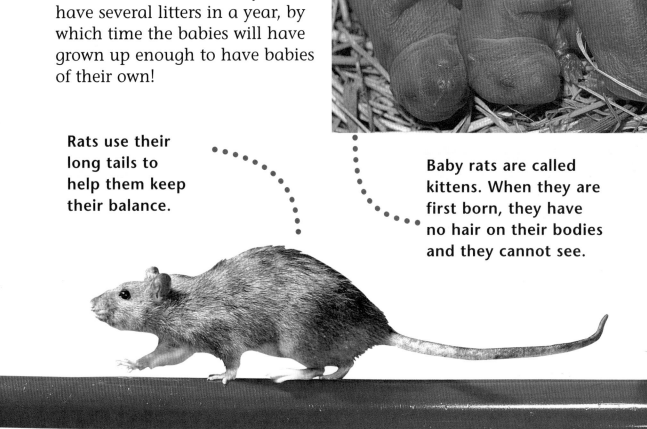

Rats use their long tails to help them keep their balance.

Baby rats are called kittens. When they are first born, they have no hair on their bodies and they cannot see.

Clever climbers

Rats are fast-moving, **agile** creatures that are good at climbing. They are very intelligent and are good at solving problems! You can teach a rat to run through a maze to its food and it will remember which route is the quickest! Their intelligence is another reason why rats are pests in the wild – they can find food easily and can escape from humans and their traps – but it is also what makes rats very good pets.

Different colours

Pet rats come in lots of different colours. Colours for rats include white, cinnamon (reddish-brown), champagne (cream), chocolate (dark brown) and blue (smoky grey-blue). Rats of specific colours are grouped into types and are often called **fancy rats**. There are also rats that do not belong to a particular type, but they still look pretty and make good pets.

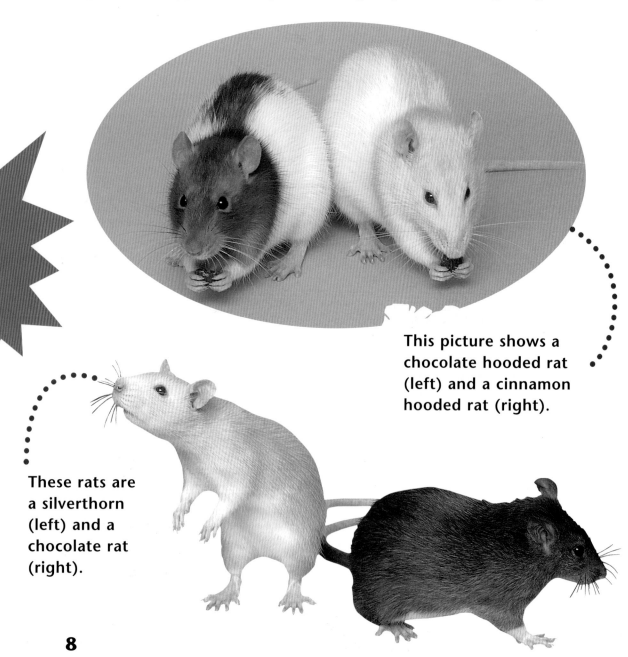

This picture shows a chocolate hooded rat (left) and a cinnamon hooded rat (right).

These rats are a silverthorn (left) and a chocolate rat (right).

8

A wide choice

There are lots of different types of fancy rat to choose from! A good way to find out more about these varieties is to get in touch with a rat society – you can find details of these at the end of the book. You could also contact your local rat club, visit some rat shows or talk to rat owners. You will soon find out that rats make excellent pets and discover that they are nothing like their wild cousins.

The rat above is a mink variegated rat.

This picture shows a Berkshire rat (top) and a hooded rat (bottom).

Are rats for you?

Some people may tell you that rats make the best small pets of all because they are so intelligent and friendly. They might even think that they are more fun to keep than cats or dogs.

As with all pets, there are good and bad things about owning rats. Here are some of the good points and not-so-good points.

Rat good points

- Rats are intelligent. They recognize their owners and love human company.
- Rats will quickly learn your routine. You may find them waiting at the front of their cage when it is time for them to be taken out!
- Rats are not truly **nocturnal**, so they are happy to be up and active when you are.
- Rats are not expensive to buy or to feed.
- Above all, rats have character. They have big personalities in small bodies. This makes them real friends – some are more like little dogs or cats!

Your rats will love to sit on your shoulder. They will probably play with your hair and might even lick your face!

Rat not-so-good points

- A rat can bite hard if it is hurt or frightened.
- Rats will chew absolutely anything they can reach from their cage.
- Some **bucks** like to mark places where they have been with a few drops of **urine**. This does not smell, but it can be off-putting for some people.
- Sadly, rats do not live long. Most of them only live for about 24 to 30 months.

Yes or no?

So, are rats for you? Having rats for pets means giving them food and water every day, cleaning out their cage every week, and giving them lots of attention. Are you really sure that you are prepared to do all these things, even when you are in a hurry or want to do something else? If the answer is yes, then you could be ready to begin keeping rats as pets. This hobby could last for many years – or even for the rest of your life!

When your rats see you coming, they will run to the front of their cage – all ready to play with you!

Rats are very friendly and trusting. Once your pets have got used to you, they will be happy to sit in your hands.

11

Choosing your rats

There are lots of things to think about when you are choosing a rat. Always take an adult with you to help you choose your pet, and if possible ask an experienced rat keeper to come along too and give you advice.

One or more?

Rats like the company of other rats. It is not exactly wrong to keep a single rat, but you will have to give your pet a lot of time and attention. A lonely rat will probably be very unhappy.

It is much better to keep two rats rather than one. They will be just as friendly with you, but they will also have each other for company when you are busy. In fact, two rats will be twice the fun! Try to choose two rats of the same age who are already used to each other. Best of all, choose two sisters or two brothers.

Rats are naturally **gregarious** – which means they enjoy the company of other rats.

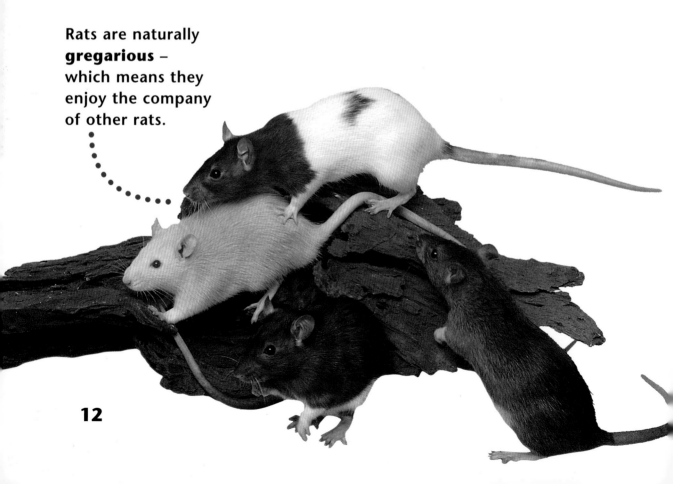

Buck or doe?

Usually, **bucks** are bigger than **does**. Bucks are also lazier, so they are probably the best choice if you want a pet that will sit quietly on your lap. The one drawback with bucks is that some of them like to mark the places they have been with a few drops of **urine**. This is a scent mark to let other rats know that your rat is around. We cannot smell it but other rats can. It is less of a problem than it sounds, but some people do not like the idea very much.

Does are usually more lively and playful than bucks. Most does do not mark places with urine, but a few of them (usually the very bossy ones!) do it just as much as bucks.

Top tips

- If you decide to keep more than one rat, make sure that all your rats are the same sex. If they are not, you could end up with far more pets than you had planned for!
- Both bucks and does make equally good pets, so the choice is up to you.
- Try to visit some rat keepers and rat shows to get to know a few bucks and does before you decide which will suit you best.

If you have two rats, they will keep each other company when you are not around.

13

What age?

It is best to choose pet rats of about eight weeks old. Older rats take longer to get used to their human owners and rats under six weeks are too young to leave their mothers. Unfortunately, many pet shop owners will not know exactly how old their rats are, or even what sex they are. However, if you take an experienced rat keeper with you, they may be able to help.

Top tip

Never buy a rat if it has a runny nose or eyes, or if it is sneezing and seems unwell.

These young rats look healthy and **alert**, with bright eyes and shiny coats. They would make excellent pets.

What to look for

There are a few basic things to look out for when you are choosing rats.

- The rats should be living in clean surroundings.
- They should have bright eyes, clean ears and a clean tail.
- Their coats should be soft, with no bald patches.
- They should be interested in you, and not nervous.

Your local rat breeder should have plenty of rats to choose from. Take a little time to get to know the rats before you choose any.

Top tip

If you are choosing a doe, make sure she has been separated from male rats since she was eight weeks old. Otherwise, she could be pregnant. It is unfair for an animal so young to breed when she is no more than a baby herself and still has a lot of growing up to do.

What do I need?

Rats can be kept in cages or tanks, but the most important thing is to give your pets plenty of room. Rats are active and playful creatures and they will make good use of whatever space you provide.

Choosing a cage

Most people keep their pet rats in a cage. A cage measuring about 60 × 40 × 40 centimetres is about right for a pair of rats, but try to get a bigger one if you can.

Many pet shops stock cages especially for rats. Look for one that is roomy and easy to clean. Cages with metal bars and plastic trays in their base are simple to keep clean. Doors and cage panels need to be secure enough to prevent the rat from escaping, so test them carefully before you buy your cage.

Top tip

Wooden cages are not ideal. Rats will eventually gnaw them to pieces. They are difficult to keep clean as **urine** soaks into the wood and makes it smelly and rotten.

Most cages have metal bars and a plastic base. Make sure the bars are narrow enough to stop a rat from squeezing through!

Top tip

Rats love to climb, so choose a cage that is tall enough to fit ramps, ladders, ropes or branches inside so that your rats can exercise and play.

Choosing a tank

Another way of keeping rats is in a glass or **perspex** tank. However, it is very important to find a suitable lid for the tank. Choose one that lets in air but does not have large enough holes for your rats to climb through! It is very important to let enough air into the tank because otherwise **condensation** (drops of water) can collect on the inside of the tank walls, making it damp. This can be dangerous to a rat's health.

Some cages are made entirely of metal. These can work well, so long as the floor is solid. Wire mesh floors are uncomfortable and can give rats sore feet.

Your rats will be happy to live in a perspex tank like this, but make sure your pets have plenty of air and the tank has a tight-fitting lid so your rats cannot escape!

The perfect place

Once you have chosen your pets' home, you will need to find the right place for it. Rats can suffer from **heat stroke** if the temperature gets too high (over 20° centigrade), so keep the cage out of direct sunlight and away from hot radiators. Rats can also become ill if they get too cold or are kept in a draught. Choose a sheltered place for their cage where they will not be too hot or too cold, and where there is not much variation in temperature.

Keep your cage on a table or a shelf, where the rats will not be bothered by other family pets.

Woodchips and shavings

You will need something to cover the floor of your rats' cage. Woodchips and shavings are usually best. Make sure that you buy them from good pet shops rather than direct from a timber yard. You do not want your woodchips and shavings to be full of nails, splinters, tea bags and other assorted rubbish! More seriously, woodchips from timber yards may contain germs from wild rats and mice that could make your pet rats ill.

The woodchips and shavings should not be too fine or dusty, or they may hurt a rat's eyes or get up its nose.

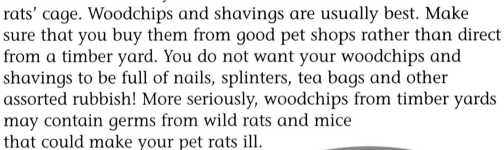

Top tip

If good woodchips are hard to find, try using cat litter pellets made from recycled paper. Some rat owners prefer to use these.

Bedding

Rats need material to make themselves a bed. You can use shredded paper for bedding, but avoid newspaper as the ink is not good for rats. Paper towels are fine – let the rats do the tearing up! Hay is also suitable. This should always be bought from a pet shop as hay straight from a farm may have fleas, **ticks** or **mites** living in it.

Bedding boxes

You may want to make a bedding box for your rats. A plant pot stuffed with bedding is fine, and so is a cardboard shoebox with a rat-sized hole cut into its side. A bedding box will give your rats somewhere private to sleep. There are endless possibilities – you will find yourself looking at things and thinking, 'I could give that to my rat to sleep in or play with.'

You can make a simple bedding box from a cardboard shoebox filled with shredded paper towels.

Toys for rats

Rats are playful and inquisitive creatures, so toys are a must. Your pets will enjoy having ladders and branches to climb on, shelves to run along and tunnels to explore. Blocks of wood will give your rats something to chew on so they can keep their teeth short. Apple and pear wood are best. You can also buy chewing blocks from your pet shop or rat breeder.

Blocks of wood are good for a rat's teeth and provide hours of chewing fun.

Climbing around

Many rat cages are fitted with shelves, ramps and ladders, but you can also give your pets some branches to climb on. Choose rough branches that are still covered with bark, as these will help to keep your rats' nails short.

Rats love climbing through, over and under things!

20

Buying and making

Many pet shops and rat breeders sell colourful plastic tunnels, slides and houses for rats to explore. You can also make your own rat toys from wide cardboard tubes and boxes with holes cut out of them. Try mixing up your pets' plastic toys with things you have made yourself to create an obstacle course. You could even try making a maze for your rats. Rats are so clever that your pets will soon find their way through the maze.

Your rats will have fun with almost anything you give them. But do not let your pets play with something they might swallow.

Not too full!

Do not fill your pets' cage so full of toys that there is not enough room for them to run around! Most of all, rats enjoy plenty of open space.

No wheels

Exercise wheels are not good for rats. They are often too small for adult rats, especially some of the hefty **bucks**. Wheels with open bars can be dangerous as rats' tails can get caught up in the bars and injured. Solid wheels are usually made of plastic so rats will chew at them. Many plastic wheels have nasty metal spikes in the middle once the plastic coating is gone. It is much better for your rats to have other toys to play with and to have lots of exercise time outside their cage.

21

Looking after your rats

Your rat cage will need to be cleaned out thoroughly once a week. Throw out all the woodchips and bedding and wipe down the cage with a mild disinfectant. You can buy safe cleaning sprays from a pet shop. Do not forget to wipe down the shelves as well as any toys or branches in the cage. When everything is completely dry, put in fresh woodchips and bedding and put all the toys, branches and shelves back inside the cage.

A weekly clean does not take long and will keep your rats' home smelling sweet. Rat **urine** can become quite smelly, so you and your family will soon notice if you do not clean the cage regularly!

Top tip

You will not need to spend much time keeping your rats clean. Rats are very clean animals and they spend a lot of time **grooming** themselves. However, rats' tails can sometimes get grubby. You can clean them with mild soap and water. Just rub the tail gently with a flannel then rinse it with clean water.

It is important to clean your rat cage every week. Otherwise it will soon start to smell.

Daily cleaning

As well as giving the cage a weekly clean, you will also have some clearing up to do every day.

- Remove any uneaten food that is left scattered around the cage, especially fruit or vegetables that can attract flies.
- Wash the food bowl.
- Check the water bottle to make sure it is clean and full of fresh water.
- Remove any **faeces** scattered about the cage.
- Scoop out any woodchips made wet with urine.
- Rats can have an annoying habit of wetting their beds. Check that your rats' bedding is clean and dry.

Washing is easiest if you have two bowls, side by side – one for washing and the other for rinsing.

Bath time

Occasionally your rats may need a bath. They will certainly need one if you decide to enter them for shows. If you treat your rats gently, bath times will be fun for all of you!

- Dip your rats into a bowl of lukewarm water and then hold them out of the water while you use a mild shampoo on their coats and tails. Be careful not to let any shampoo get into their eyes.
- Rinse your pets off in clean warm water and dry them with a towel.
- Make sure your rats are completely dry and comfortable before they return to their cage.

After you have dried your rats, they may like to scamper around a bit to get warmed up!

23

Food for rats

Your rats' basic diet should be a mixture of grains and cereals that you can buy from a pet shop. Rat food is sold in boxes or packets or even loose. However, do make sure that the food is meant for rats. Gerbil and hamster food contains a lot of sunflower seeds and nuts, which rats love, but can cause sore spots on a rat's skin. It is much better to feed your rats a proper rat food, and give them an occasional sunflower seed or nut as a treat. Follow the feeding instructions on the packet as a guideline to how much you should feed your pets.

Healthy extras

You can add a few extra **ingredients** to your rats' basic diet. Wholemeal bread or toast, plain breakfast cereals, cooked rice or noodles and cooked potato will all be appreciated by your pets – but don't overdo it! Your rats will also enjoy chewing on a dog biscuit – this is a tasty way to keep their teeth healthy.

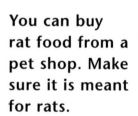

You can buy rat food from a pet shop. Make sure it is meant for rats.

Fruit and vegetables

Fruit and vegetables are good for rats.

- The best fruits are apples, although some rats love melon, cherries and peaches! It is best to avoid very acidic fruits like oranges.
- Carrots, lettuce, cabbage and celery are good vegetables to give your rats.
- Do not feed onions or very strong tasting vegetables to your pets. Start by giving your rats small amounts, to see which kind they prefer.

Feeding times

You can choose when to feed your rats, but it is usually best to feed them in the evening with a top-up in the morning for breakfast if they need it. Rats will store extra food that they are not hungry enough to eat. Large stores mean that you are overfeeding them!

Most rats love nibbling on fresh fruit and vegetables.

Safety first

Rats can get tummy upsets from eating too much fruit or too many vegetables. Stick to very small amounts and only give your rats fruit or vegetables every other day.

Rats are enthusiastic eaters! They often climb right inside their feeding bowl.

Tasty treats

You can buy various treats for rats. These may be bars of cereals to be attached to the cage, tasty yogurt drops or small biscuits. Rats enjoy these, but you can offer them lots of other things too. Your rats will almost certainly enjoy a small taste of biscuit, chocolate, cake, or even ice-cream – but do not give them too much! You know how bad it is to eat too much of these things, but your rats do not. A tiny taste now and again is okay but it is up to you not to let your rats get fat or ill by eating too many of the wrong foods.

Top tip

Generally speaking, if you like eating something, your rats will probably like it too!

Your rats will probably love a small taste of ice cream, but never give them this much!

Pet shops sell a range of healthy treats like this.

A bony treat!

A good tasty treat for rats is a small bone with a little meat still on it. Rats enjoy meat and chewing on the bone is good for their teeth. The bone can also provide valuable **calcium** which will help your pets to have strong teeth and bones. A clean, cooked bone can be left in the cage for a day or so, but meaty bones must be removed after one day, as they will soon go bad and start to smell.

Water bottles

Finally, and very importantly, rats should always have fresh water to drink. A water bottle hung from the cage wires is best. You can also buy a clip to hang a water bottle from the lid of a tank. Water bottles work by letting drops of water flow whenever a rat licks the end of the spout. That way, your pets can get enough to drink without their bottle dripping into the cage.

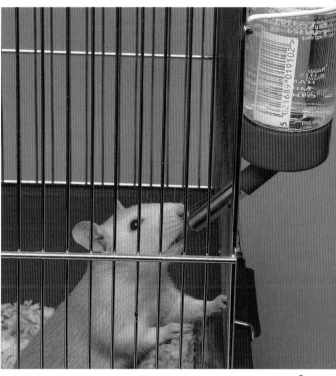

Holidays

Rats need daily care. If you are going away, make sure you have arranged for someone to look after your pets.

- Find a friend or neighbour who knows and likes rats.
- Ask them to visit your rats every day, to give them food and water and clean out their cage.
- You should leave clear instructions about what to feed your pets and who to ring if there is an emergency.

Rats need to drink lots of water. Remember to fill their bottle with new, fresh water every day.

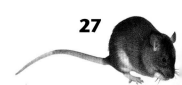

Happy and healthy?

You need to check your pets regularly to make sure they are fit and well. Are your rats eating and drinking properly and do they seem lively and **alert**? When you clean out the cage, check your rats' faeces. They should not be very runny or too hard.

Daily checks

While you are handling your rats, feel them all over to make sure there are no lumps, bumps or swellings on their bodies. Check that your pets' coats are clean and soft, with no sore places or specks of dirt from fleas. Make sure that the skin on their ears and tails is clean and smooth, not rough and scaly.

Top tip

If you see something that could be a problem, tell your parents or another adult. They can help you decide whether you need to take your pet to the vet.

Feel each rat's body gently to make sure it has no fleas or **ticks** and no lumps or swellings.

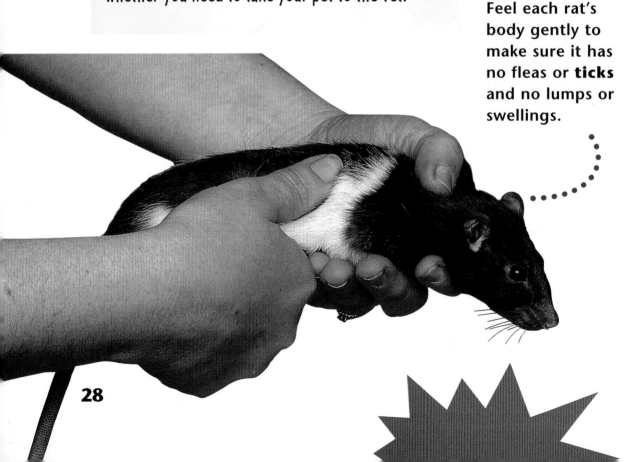

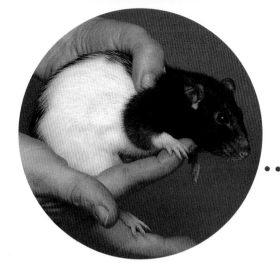

Check that your rats' nails are not getting too long. You might need to have them trimmed.

Keep an eye on your pets' nails – they sometimes need trimming. Until you are used to rats, your vet will do this for you. Also, check your pets' teeth. Rats' teeth keep growing all the time and if your pets are not chewing enough, their teeth can become **overgrown**. If a rat's teeth become too long they can even stop it from feeding properly. You can find out more about health problems on pages 36 to 41.

This rat's teeth are the correct length. But if a rat is not chewing enough, its teeth might start growing too long. You will need to take your pet to the vet to have its teeth clipped.

Watch out!

Here are some things to look out for when you are playing with your rats.

- Watch how your rats move around. A limp or an unusual way of walking may mean that your rat has been injured or is in pain.
- Are your pets getting fatter or thinner? A change in weight can be a sign of a serious health problem.
- Is one of your rats holding its head on one side? This may mean it has an ear problem.

Handling your rats

Pet rats are not wild animals. They have been **domesticated** so they are happy to live with people. But this does not mean you will be able to handle your rats immediately. As with every friendship, human or animal, it will take a little time to get to know each other and feel confident together.

Your rats will probably take a while to explore their new home and settle in comfortably.

A new home

When you first take your rats home, give them time to settle in before you try to play with them or handle them.

Some rats settle in quicker than others. Some will be standing up at the bars demanding your attention as soon as they have explored their cage. Others will be quite shy and will have to be coaxed out of their cage. Food is always a great way of making friends! Quietly offer a tasty titbit and let the rat take it from your fingers. If you have a very shy rat, you may need to put a titbit near the front of the cage and sit quietly while it plucks up the courage to take it.

Top tip

Do not try to pick up your pets straightaway. Remember that your hand will look enormous to a rat, so it has to learn that you will not hurt it.

Slowly does it

Take some time to allow your rats to get used to your voice and your hands. Your pets will have had a lot of changes in their short lives and they will need to feel confident. Soon they will be taking food from you – first through the bars of their cage and then directly from your hand. They may even start putting their little feet on the palm of your hand while they take their food. This sort of confidence means that a rat is ready to be handled.

You will seem like a giant to your rats! Talk to them softly and let them get used to the sound of your voice.

Soon, your rats will be happy to take a titbit from your fingers.

Other pets

- You will need to be very careful about letting your rats meet other pets. Most cats and dogs could kill a rat if they wanted to. Take care when you introduce them and never leave them alone together.
- Rats can also badly frighten or even kill some other pets. Do not let them near hamsters or gerbils, even if they are in their cages. It may be too upsetting for the smaller animal.

Picking up your rat

Never pick up a rat by its tail. This is very frightening for your pet and may even injure it. Pick up a rat by putting one hand over its back and scooping it up into your other hand. This means that it will be sitting on one of your hands with your other hand over it. Stroke it and speak softly to it and try not to do anything too suddenly.

At first, a rat may not seem to like being handled, but it is important to hold it as much as you can so that it gets used to being held. If it wriggles and needs to be stopped from jumping or falling you can steady it by holding the very base of its tail next to its bottom.

Offer a treat, such as a trickle of ice cream on your fingers. Your pet will soon learn that handling means nice things are going to happen!

Pick up a rat by putting one hand on its back and scooping it up with your other hand.

A rat will like being held against your body while you support its bottom with your other hand.

32

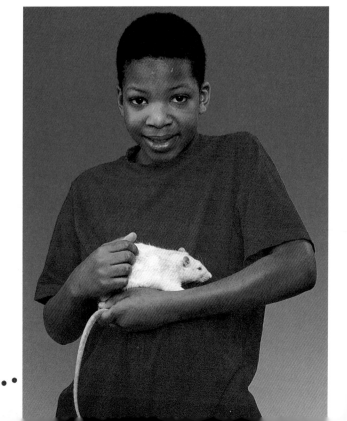

Top tip

If your rats try to hide in your clothing – let them! Rats love being carried around in their owner's jumper or T-shirt, so it can be a good way of getting your pets used to riding around on you.

Contented chuckles

As your rats become more confident, let them sit on your shoulder. This is a favourite place for many rats, and they will happily sit with you while you watch TV or walk around the house. Often a happy rat will 'chuckle' and make a tooth-grinding noise which can sound quite loud when it is right in your ear! Some rats even lick their owner's face. They have very soft velvety tongues and very tickly whiskers!

Playtime

Try to set aside some time every day for your pets to play outside their cage. It is best to keep your rats in just one or two rooms where you can stay with them and make sure that they do not get into any trouble. You can give your pets some tubes and boxes to play in, but they will mainly enjoy just being out and exploring.

Top tip

You should always remember to wash your hands after handling a rat.

Your rats will love to run along the backs of sofas and chairs and inspect whoever is sitting there!

Rat-proofing a room

Before you let your rats out to play, you will need to make sure that they cannot get hurt. You will also have to keep things safe from your rats! Be careful that there is nothing in their reach that they can chew to bits.

Inspect the room for any places where a rat could get stuck or lost. The best way to do this is to pretend to be a rat! Lie down flat on the floor and ask yourself what you can see that is rat-sized and might seem worth exploring. Look for gaps in fireplaces and behind cupboards, or cracks in floorboards. These will all need blocking up. Check also that your pets cannot get inside furniture. A number of pet rats meet a sudden death by being sat on in sofas or chairs.

Electricity alert

Rats love chewing things. Electric cables and TV, video and computer leads all look like tasty things for a rat to chew on. This could be very dangerous for your pet because it might get an electric shock that could kill it. If there are some cables that cannot be moved, fit protective cable sleeves round them to stop them from being chewed.

Before you let your rats out to play, make sure there are no electric cables lying around.

Chewing trouble

Rats can be quite destructive if they are not watched. A favourite trick is to chew any material they can reach from their cage. So do not leave your best jumper near your pets' cage. They may reach out and drag it in! And if a rat disappears behind the curtains when it is out playing, it may well be chewing holes in them!

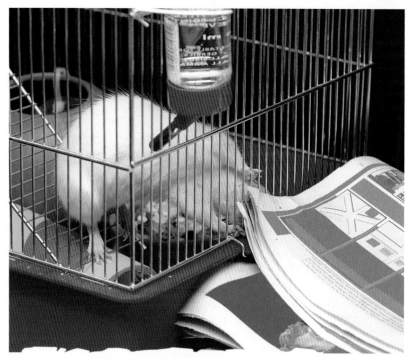

If you leave anything close to your pets' cage, your rats will try to find a way of dragging it inside!

Top tips

- Rats often steal things. This can be amusing but rats are not clever enough to know when something is really harmful.
- Check your room to see what is lying around and remove any precious objects or things that would be bad for your rats to chew on.

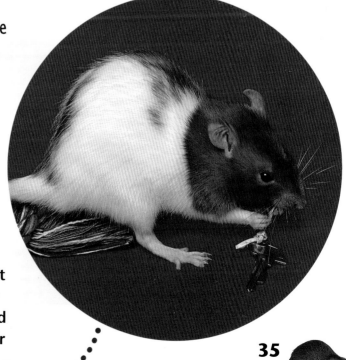

Rats take a fancy to objects that they can pick up and carry. Key rings, sweet wrappers, pens and even jewellery may all find their way into a rat's hiding place!

35

Some health problems

Rats are quite healthy little animals but there are a few illnesses and problems that rat owners need to recognize. Because rats are very small, they can get ill very fast – so having an experienced vet nearby is important.

Colds

Runny eyes and nose, wheezing and sneezing may well mean that your rat has a cold. Rats can catch colds if they are in a draught, if the temperature drops dramatically, or if they are near another rat with a cold. Sometimes the liquid from your rat's eyes and nose may be pink and look like blood, but it is not. Colds can be quite serious to rats, so take your pet to the vet. The vet will give your pet an **antibiotic** injection to help fight the cold. You must also keep it away from other rats to stop them catching the cold too. Make sure your rat is warm and is drinking lots of water.

If your rat becomes seriously ill, take it straight to the vet.

Skin problems

Spots and sores on a rat's skin can be painful and itchy. There are two main causes of skin problems in rats. The first is diet. Your rat may have been eating too many sunflower seeds or nuts. If this is the case, replace its normal diet with very simple food for a few days, such as boiled rice and plain bread. If your rat's skin starts to look better, then diet was probably the cause.

The second cause of sores, scabs and bald patches are **mites**. These are tiny **parasites** that live in some animals' coats. They may have come from hay or straw or from another rat. If you have recently bought a new rat, you should ask your vet to check it for mites. Your vet will give you a special shampoo to kill the mites. Change all the bedding and woodchips in your pet's cage and do not let it near other rats until it is clear of mites.

Tummy troubles

- **Diarrhoea** is often caused by too much fruit or too many vegetables or by too many unhealthy treats. This is easily put right. Just feed your rat a very plain diet for a few days.
- Sometimes, a rat can develop diarrhoea if it is travelling or being moved from place to place. This normally settles down on its own.
- If your rat is suffering from **constipation** it will have very hard **faeces** that are difficult to pass. Constipation can be very painful. It is often caused by too much dried food. Feeding your rat with a little lettuce or salad greens can improve things.

Normal rat faeces should be quite soft and **cylindrical** in shape. If they are runny or very dry, your rat has a problem.

37

Ear problems

If your rat starts to hold its head tilted to one side there is probably something wrong with its ears. Your rat may even have trouble balancing. Your vet will give you some ear drops to help clear the **infection**. Rats usually recover well, although some bad ear infections may leave a rat with a permanently tilted head.

Lumps and bumps

Many rats develop lumps and bumps. Sometimes these may be soft and full of pus. These are called **abscesses** and are caused by an infection developing around a wound or a bite. Abscesses can be drained and cleaned and usually heal up very well.

Your vet will be able to give you advice about what to look for when examining your rats.

Other lumps may be harder masses of fatty skin. Most of these lumps are **benign**, which means they are harmless. They can often be removed by an operation. Sadly, rats sometimes develop **cancerous tumours**. These are often just like the benign fatty lumps, but they feel harder. They grow fast and eventually make the rat very ill. If this happens, you should talk to your vet about whether it would be best to have your rat **put to sleep**.

Eye problems

- If your rat has watery or runny eyes, ask an adult to help you bathe them with a soft tissue soaked in warm water. There may just be a speck of dust in your rat's eye.
- If the trouble comes back after bathing the eyes, it could be an infection. You will need to take your rat to the vet for some antibiotics.

Teeth problems

A rat's teeth keep on growing throughout its life, so your pets will need lots of hard things to gnaw on to wear down their teeth. Sometimes, a rat's teeth can grow so long that it cannot eat properly and starts to lose weight. If this happens, your vet can clip your rat's teeth to the right length. Your rat will not like it, but it will not hurt.

Top tip

Make sure you give your pets lots of hard blocks of wood and other things to chew on to keep their teeth the right length.

A rat's teeth keep growing all the time. This rat has lost one of its upper teeth so its lower tooth has not worn down and has grown extremely long.

Too hot

If your rats' cage is left in direct sunlight or too close to a hot radiator, your pets may become overheated and suffer from **heat stroke**. They will look uncomfortable and distressed and their breathing will become rapid and shallow. Quickly move the cage to cooler surroundings and encourage your rats to drink cool water. If your rats collapse, wrap them in cool (not ice cold) damp towels and take them to the vet.

Too cold

If your rats become really cold, they may suffer from **hypothermia**. They will seem very slow and sluggish and may even collapse. Their bodies will be hunched up and feel cold to the touch. The best thing to do is to pop your pets inside your shirt so your body temperature heats them up gently. If your rats do not show signs of getting better in ten minutes, take them to the vet straightaway.

Top tip

If a rat becomes too cold, a little drink of warm milk or water will help to increase its body temperature.

If one of your rats develops hypothermia, you need to act fast. You could try taking it to a warm place and wrapping it up in a towel or blanket.

Danger signs

Watch out for these danger signs. They might mean that one of your rats is very ill.

- Your rat is sitting hunched up as if it is very uncomfortable. Its eyes may be half closed or it may be trembling. Its coat may look scruffy because it is not grooming itself.

- Your rat cannot walk without falling over. It may have a severe ear infection.
- Your rat has difficulty breathing, and is gasping and wheezing. This may mean that the rat has **pneumonia**.

If your rat is looking more scruffy than normal, it may be a sign that your pet is unwell.

If your rat has any of these signs, you should contact your vet immediately.

Accidents can happen

Sometimes rats get broken legs. If this happens, you will need to take your pet to a vet very quickly. The vet will decide whether an operation is necessary to help mend the leg. Sometimes it may be necessary to **amputate** (cut off) a leg. Rats cope surprisingly well with only three legs. Occasionally a rat may have to be put to sleep if its injuries are too bad.

In spite of these possible illnesses, you will probably find that your rats are healthy and active little creatures for most of their lives. However, a rat's life is short – only about two and a half years – so it will not be long before you have to think about your rat as an old animal.

Growing old

Old rats need special care. They feel the cold more and are less active and **agile** than younger rats. It is a good idea to remove any ladders and climbing toys from their cage, as their balance may not be very good.

Give an old rat a quiet life with lots of gentle care and affection. It will still have a lot to enjoy even if it is not as lively as it used to be. Even though it is old and slow, your rat will still be a friend who likes to sit on your shoulder.

Once a rat is over two years old, it will probably start to look old.

A peaceful end

Some old rats die peacefully in their sleep without ever becoming really ill. Others get lots of little illnesses, aches and pains. These can mean that an old rat's life is no longer very enjoyable.

If your rat is old and sick and near the end of its life, you may decide that it is a good idea to talk to your vet about having it put to sleep. The injection does not hurt, it just makes your pet feel sleepy. Before you can count to ten, your rat will be asleep and its heart will have stopped beating.

Saying goodbye

It is hard to lose a pet that you have loved. It can seem very unfair that your rat has lived for such a short time. However, there are some things that you need to remember.

It can help to have a special burial place for your pet and maybe plant a flower or a shrub on it.

- It is not your fault, or the vet's fault, that your pet has died. It is just a hard fact that rats do not live long.
- When a pet dies, it is perfectly normal for people, adults as well as children, to cry for a while.
- Eventually the pain will pass and you will be left with happy memories of your pet. Maybe you will soon think about having another rat to look after and enjoy?

Keeping a record

It is fun to keep a record of your pet rats. Buy a big scrapbook and fill it with notes and photos. Then you can look back at it and remind yourself of all the things you and your pets did together. Your rat scrapbook can also include general information about rats and how to care for them.

A special diary

Of course, pride of place in your scrapbook will go to your own rats. You could start with the very first photo taken of them when they came to live with you. Were they really those tiny kits? Or what about the first time you held them? Or when they first sat on your shoulder? Or when Mum or Grandma were brave enough to hold them?

You can note down special events in the lives of your pets, such as the first time they explored your room or the first time you gave them a bath. You can also make a note of the funny things your rats do when they are eating or playing.

Choosing which pictures to put in your scrapbook can be a lot of fun. Maybe you could ask other people which ones they like best too.

Useful information

You can collect articles and information about rats and rat care and stick them into your scrapbook. They will soon build up into a good store of tips and guidance. You can also keep lists of your friends and contacts in rat clubs, the dates of shows and useful web sites about rats and how to look after them.

Rat shows

You may decide to show your rats. Societies such as the National Fancy Rat Society in the UK and the Australian Rat Fanciers Society in Australia have junior memberships and junior classes at shows. Maybe your rats will win rosettes that you can keep in your scrapbook!

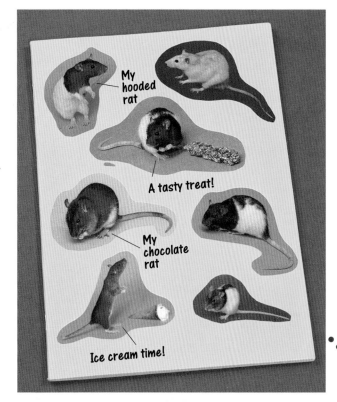

My hooded rat

A tasty treat!

My chocolate rat

Ice cream time!

When you have finished adding pictures to your scrapbook, it may be a good idea to label them. Otherwise, in years to come, you may forget what each picture is showing.

Your scrapbook should help to make sure that you never forget the special times that you and your rats enjoyed together.

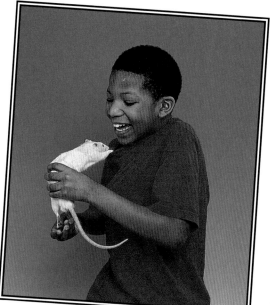

45

Glossary

abscess   soft lump filled with pus
agile   able to move quickly and easily
alert   lively and interested in everything
amputate   to cut off a leg or an arm
antibiotic   medicine that fights infection
benign   harmless or not dangerous
breed   to mate and produce young
buck   male rat
calcium   a substance that is good for building strong teeth and bones
cancerous   caused by cancer. Cancer is a disease that destroys the body's healthy cells
condensation   water that collects as drops on a cold surface
constipation   a problem caused by hard faeces (poo) that makes it difficult to go to the toilet
cylindrical   shaped like a tube
diarrhoea   runny faeces (poo)
doe   female rat
domesticate   to tame an animal, so that it can live with people
faeces   solid waste matter (poo) passed out of the body
fancy rats   rats with special markings or colours, recognized as a particular type by rat societies
gregarious   sociable, or fond of company
groom   to clean an animal's coat; animals often groom themselves
heat stroke   illness caused by getting too hot
hypothermia   illness caused by getting too cold
illegal   against the law
infection   an illness that makes part of the body fill with pus

ingredient   part of a food or meal
kitten   baby rat
litter   a number of baby rats born together
mammal   animal with fur or hair on its body that feeds its babies with milk
mature   to become adult
mite   small creature that lives on another animal's skin and sucks its blood
nocturnal   active at night
overgrown   grown too long
parasites   small creatures like fleas, ticks or worms that live on or inside another animal
perspex   clear, strong plastic
pest   a creature that causes problems for people, often by carrying diseases
pneumonia   an illness where the lungs become infected and fill with fluid
pus   thick yellow fluid inside an infected part of the body
put to sleep   give a sick animal an injection to help it die peacefully and without pain
rodent   animal with strong front teeth for gnawing
scavenge   to hunt for food
tick   small creature that lives on another animal's skin and sucks its blood
tumour   lump or growth
urine   liquid passed out of the body containing water and waste substances
vermin   animals that are pests, such as wild rats and mice
warm-blooded   used to describe an animal that can keep its body at the same tempreture

Useful addresses

Most countries have national rat societies, which give helpful advice on caring for your pets, and have members all over the country. As well as these large organizations there are also smaller rat clubs. Look in your telephone book for the address of your local rat club, or ask in your local library, pet shop or veterinary surgery. Joining a club is a great way to learn about rats and to meet new friends!

The National Fancy Rat Society
PO Box 24207, London SE9 5ZF, United Kingdom
http://www.nfrs.org/

The National Fancy Rat Society can provide you with lots of information about rats and how to care for them. They also have a calendar of rat shows throughout the country.

Rat & Mouse Club of America
13075 Sprindale Street, PMB 302, Westminster, CA92683, USA
http://www.rmca.org/

The Rat & Mouse Club of America will help you learn about how to look after your rats properly. They also hold regular rat-related events.

Australian Rat Fanciers Society
http://www.ausrfs.org.au/

The Australian Rat Fanciers Society has branches all over the country. Check their website for more information.

Australian Mouse and Rat Information Service (AMRIS)
PO Box 4248, Ringwood, Victoria, Australia 3134

AMRIS campaigns to improve the way people treat rats, mice and other rodents.

More books to read

There are not many books about rats written for young readers. These books are not specially written for children but should be enjoyed by rat owners of all ages.

The Proper Care of Fancy Rats, Nick Mays (TFH Publications, 1993)
Your First Fancy Rat, Nick Mays (Kingdom Books, 1996)

47

Index